RUBANK EDUCATIONAL LIBRARY No. 160

Selected Studies

Advanced Etudes, Scales and Arpeggios in All Major and Minor Keys

by H. Voxman

ADVANCED ETUDES

SCALES AND ARPEGGIOS

SPECIAL STUDIES

RUBANK®

HAL•LEONARD®
CORPORATION
7777 W. BLUEMOUND RD. P.O. BOX 13819 MILWAUKEE, WI 53213

C Major

GALLAY

Adagio cantabile

A Minor

BLAZHEVICH

Moderato

F Major

DUHEM

BELCKE

D Minor

9

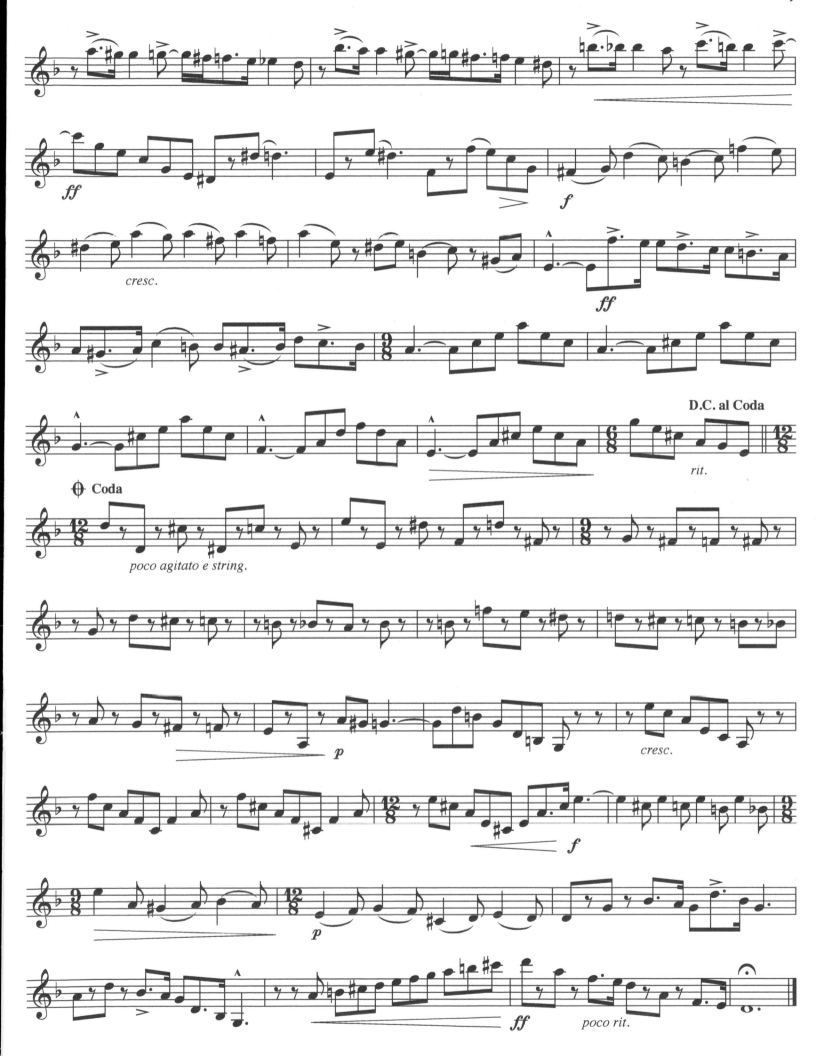

G Major

Larghetto cantabile

MÜLLER

Allegro moderato

E Minor

BÖHME

Valse lentement

B♭ Major

GATTI

BÖHME

G Minor

BOHME

BLAZHEVICH

D Major

GATTI

ROSSARI

poco rall.   a tempo

f

B Minor

ROSSARI

E♭ Major

PIETZSCH

Adagio cantabile

BLAZHEVICH

C Minor

CAPRICCIO

St. JACOME

Allegretto

A Major

Andante con moto

BLAZHEVICH

As fast as technique permits

F# Minor

BÖHME

A♭ Major

DUHEM

Adagio cantabile

BÖHME

F Minor

BLAZHEVICH

Allegro molto (quasi valse)

GATTI

Allegro mosso

E Major

FEDOROW

BLAZHEVICH

C# Minor

ROSSARI

BLAZHEVICH

D♭ Major

BÖHME

ROSSARI

B♭ Minor

BÖHME

SCHERZO

BAGANTZ

B Major

BIMBONI

Tempo di polacca

FEDOROW

G# Minor

BAGANTZ

Andante con spirito

poco a poco dim.

morendo e rallentando

ROSSARI

Poco agitato (Allegro)

F# Major

DIEPPO

BLAZHEVICH

D# Minor

BLAZHEVICH

BLAZHEVICH

C# Major

ROSSARI

JOHANSON

A# Minor

ROSSARI

Allegretto comodo

BLAZHEVICH

Velocity

St. JACOME
(adapted)

Scales

The use of a metronome with the following studies is highly recommended.

C MAJOR

A MINOR (melodic form) *

F MAJOR

D MINOR

* All minor scale exercises should also be practiced in the harmonic form.

G MAJOR

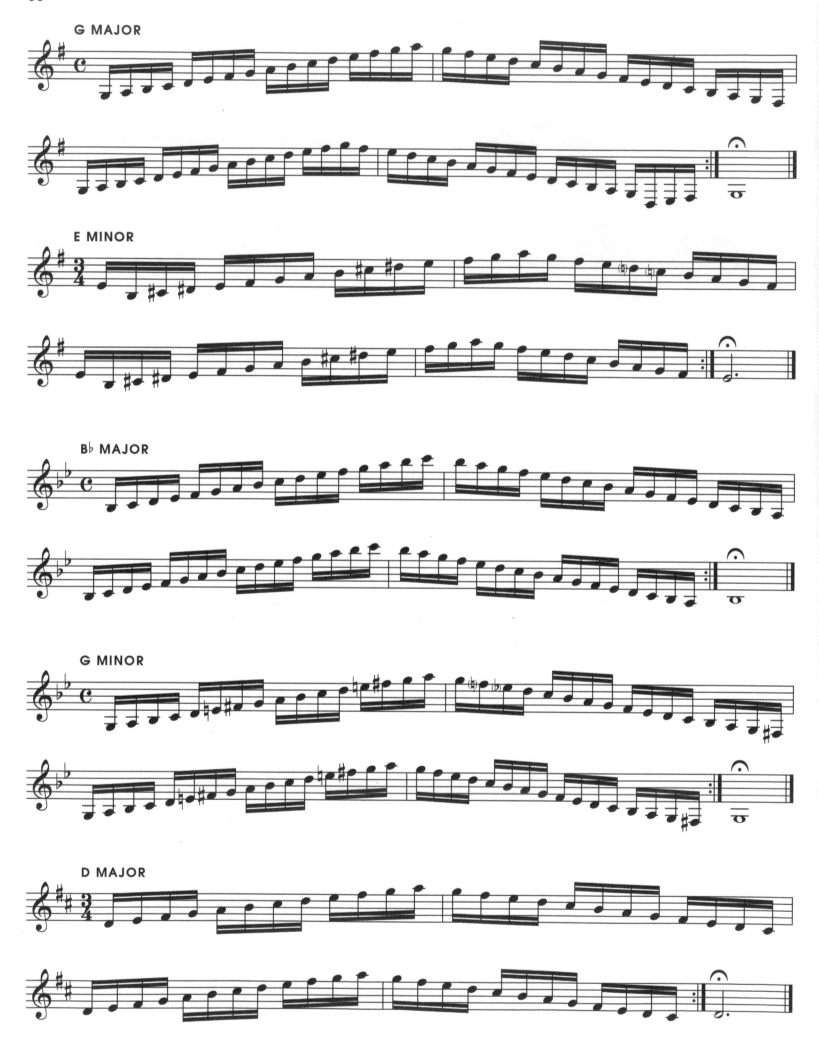

E MINOR

Bb MAJOR

G MINOR

D MAJOR

58

A♭ MAJOR

F MINOR

E MAJOR

C♯ MINOR

D♭ MAJOR

Chromatic Study

BÖHME

Arpeggios

64

C# MAJOR

A# MINOR

B MAJOR

G# MINOR

F# MAJOR

D# MINOR

C# MAJOR

A# MINOR

Arpeggio of the augmented 5th

Interval Studies

BAGANTZ

ARBAN

Apply to exercises 3 – 10:

CORNETTE

Tonguing Studies

CHAVANNE

Allegro ma non troppo
Single and double tonguing

Allegro moderato

Single and triple tonguing

Cadenza Studies